Life in Bible Times

By Robert Henderson
and Ian Gould

Consultant editor
Mary Alice Jones

Rand McNally & Company

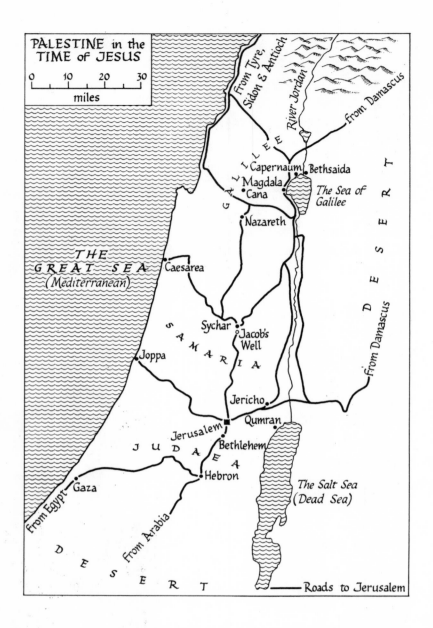

PALESTINE in the TIME of JESUS

0 10 20 30
miles

From Tyre, Sidon & Antioch

River Jordan

From Damascus

GALILEE

Capernaum · Bethsaida

Magdala
· Cana

The Sea of Galilee

· Nazareth

THE GREAT SEA
(Mediterranean)

Caesarea

S A M A R I A

Sychar · Jacob's Well

From Damascus

Joppa

Jericho ·

Jerusalem · Qumran

Bethlehem

J U D A E A

· Hebron

From Egypt · Gaza

From Arabia

D E S E R T

The Salt Sea
(Dead Sea)

D E S E R T

—— Roads to Jerusalem

Designed by Marc Sale and Illustrated by Alex Bennett

Published jointly with W. & R. Chambers, Ltd., Edinburgh, 1967

© R. Henderson and I. Gould, 1967

Library of Congress Catalog Card Number: 67-18286   Printed in U.S.A.

ISBN 528-87765-8

First Paperback Printing, 1977

Contents

Palestine, the "Promised Land"

The Jewish people had grown up in this little land behind natural barriers. Palestine was shut off from the north by mountains; from the east by the deep valley of the river Jordan and by the desert; from the south by more desert; and from the west by a sea which the Jews still feared.

WHAT A SMALL LAND Palestine is! It is only 150 miles long and 50 miles wide—slightly less than the size of the State of New Jersey, one of our smallest states.

Yet to us it is one of the most important lands on earth, for there Jesus lived all his life. To the Jews of Jesus' day, too, it was full of history. Every hill and valley, every town and village, almost every well and stream, had its ancient story. Jesus himself was always reminded of his nation's past and was proud of it.

To the Israelites the most amazing thing about the Promised Land was its climate. As one old writer said, "Egypt drinks from the Nile, Babylon from the rivers, but things are ordered otherwise in the land of Israel. There the men sleep in their beds and God sends the rain down to them."

From May to October there was continual sunshine, but the morning dew and the winds off the sea kept the heat bearable. From December to February was the cold rainy season, but even then there was a great deal of sunshine.

When rain did fall, it fell heavily, but in some years the rains did not come and there was drought. The "former rains" of October and November softened the parched ground enough for plowing to begin and brought the wild flowers into bloom. The "latter rains" of March and April were awaited just as eagerly. Only the moisture they brought could save the growing crops when the east wind from the desert blew in with withering dust and heat.

When Joshua led the Israelites into Canaan, what a good land it must have seemed after forty years of wandering in the desert! No longer did they have to live in tents, moving from place to place to find drinking water and new pastures for their sheep and goats. No longer did they have to try to grow little crops on patches of poor earth before moving on to their next camp.

Here in Canaan, the Promised Land, there was good soil that could be used year after year for growing crops. There was usually enough rain, too, and plenty of wood and stone for building. So they settled down in one place and learned how to build houses and grow crops there. The Canaanite people stayed on in the land, and the Israelites copied some of their ways.

Nomads and shepherds

THERE WERE SOME ISRAELITES who did not settle down in Canaan to farm the land. They believed that men could not remain true to God if they lived more comfortable lives in houses and owned fields and vineyards. So they lived their lives in very much the same way as Abraham and his tribe had done.

Most Jews, even centuries later in Jesus' time, thought of the time of Abraham as "the good old days," so let us see what life was like then.

Abraham and his tribe must have looked like this when they traveled with their flocks. Both men and women wear loose cloaks made of strips of brightly-colored woolen cloth sewed together. The men wear sandals, the women, calf-length boots. The women have long hair reaching below their shoulders, with a white band around the forehead and curls in front of the ears. The men's hair is short, and they have carefully trimmed and pointed beards.

The men carry their weapons—except one who is playing the lyre, a kind of small harp which was the favorite musical instrument. The asses carry all the heavy belongings. Most important are the water bags, made of animal skins and covered with woolen cloth in colored patterns. You can also see two sets of bellows for metalworking, for these men have learned how to make metal tools and weapons.

In the time of Jesus, shepherds and their flocks were still a common sight on the hillsides. When Jesus said, "I am the good shepherd; I know my sheep and my sheep know me . . . and I lay down my life for the sheep," everyone knew what he meant.

For the shepherd lived with his flock. He guarded them by day on the open pastures and by night in the rough stone-wall folds. He protected the sheep against foxes, wolves, jackals, bears, and (in Old Testament times) lions. If a sheep was attacked, the shepherd had to rescue two legs or a piece of an ear to prove to his master that the sheep had not been lost by carelessness.

The shepherd really did come to know each animal, and they all knew him. The sheep followed him wherever he led them because they trusted him.

They made camp at an oasis, where there was drinking water and some good soil. They dug little patches of ground and sowed seed—probably a kind of rye. Of course, the people at the oasis could not move until the crop was gathered in. Meanwhile, some men of the tribe took their flocks to find nearby pastures—where the animals had to be guarded all the time against wild beasts. When the animals had eaten all they could find at one pasture, the shepherds moved their tents and flocks to another. After the harvest, the whole tribe moved off to another oasis.

Above all, however, Abraham and his tribe were shepherds who lived in tents. Their goats supplied milk and also hair from which cloth was woven. Their broadtailed sheep provided meat, skins, and wool for clothes.

Farmers

Plowing began after the "former rains" of October and November. The plow was made of wood with a point coated with iron. It was drawn by two oxen, for the law forbade "unequal yoking"—that is, an ox and ass yoked together. It had only one handle, which left the plowman's other hand free to use the ox goad. On good soil the land was plowed after sowing, but rough soil was plowed both before sowing and afterwards. On the terraces of hillsides, where there was no room for a plow, men loosened the soil with a mattock, a kind of pick.

WHEN THE ISRAELITES settled in Palestine some Canaanite people stayed on. From them the Israelites learned ways of farming which continued almost to our own day. The most important crops were the vine, the olive, and grain. Vines were grown on the hillsides, which were usually terraced. Olives, which require little water, were grown on shallow or rocky soil. Grain crops—wheat, barley, and rye—were grown in the valleys and on the lower slopes of hills.

Wheat was grown on the best ground. Even here, however, there were stones and thorns—as we know from the parable of the sower. In fact, large stones were considered a sign of fertile ground. It was too difficult to move the largest, but stones that could be handled were taken to the side of the field to make a boundary wall. This was often the home of snakes and scorpions. Barley, for the poor man's bread, was sown on ground which was not quite good enough for wheat; rye was grown on the poorest land.

Wheat might be sown in rows, but most seed was sown "broadcast": that is, a man walked up and down the field with a basket of seed and scattered it by hand as evenly as he could. However careful he was, some was wasted on the roadway, on stony ground, or among the thorns at the edge of the field.

Harvesting was tiring work. Men either pulled up the grain by the roots or cut it with sickles edged with flints or iron. They grasped a handful of stalks, cut them just below the ears, gathered several handfuls in one arm, and laid them on the ground behind. Women followed and bound the sheaves with straw.

Then the sheaves were taken to the threshing floor to separate the kernels from the stalks. There they might be beaten with flails—long sticks—or animals might be driven over the grain to trample it. Usually, however, a threshing "machine" was used. This might be a "sledge" (made of boards, studded underneath with stones or metal) or a "cart" (a frame on rollers fitted with metal disks). These "machines" were weighted with boulders and pulled by asses or oxen around and around the threshing floor. The animals were blindfolded so that they did not become dizzy.

When the wind blew in the late afternoon or evening, winnowing began. The mixed pile was thrown into the air, first with a fork and then with a shovel. The chaff blew away; the straw fell a short distance off and was saved for feeding the animals; the grain fell at the feet of the winnower. It was then sifted by hand to remove pieces of stone.

Work in olive groves

Harvesting was not difficult either; the branches were shaken or the berries were knocked down with long poles and gathered in baskets.

Olive berries were eaten, either fresh or pickled, with bread—but they were chiefly used to produce oil. In very early times olive berries may have been trodden like grapes, but later there were three ways of obtaining oil. The best oil was beaten oil, obtained by pounding the berries in a mortar (a large shallow stone dish), and then gently shaking the pulp in wicker baskets. Second-quality oil came from pressing this pulp in the wicker baskets under a heavy beam lever weighted with stones. Third-quality oil was produced in an oil mill. In this a long pivoted wooden beam turned an upright stone wheel over the berries which lay on a flat circular stone. This flat stone was grooved, and the oil flowed along the grooves into a vat at the side.

FOR THE EARLY ISRAELITES the olive was so important that in one fable we are told that it was chosen the King of the Trees. In Jesus' lifetime it was just as important as in those earlier days.

The olive was a very easy tree to cultivate. New wood had to be grafted onto an older fruit-bearing root stock and allowed to mature for some years. Then a tree would bear crops for centuries with little attention. A good tree would yield about twelve to fifteen gallons of oil every second year.

Oil was also used for washing the face each day and as a dressing for the hair. Anointing—pouring oil over the head—was a mark of honor. Guests were anointed; so were priests, kings, some prophets, and the dead. "Christ," "The Lord's Anointed One," came to mean "He that cometh in the name of the Lord"—*the* prophet, priest, and king.

Olive oil was used for food and for light. Where we might use lard in cooking, the Jewish woman used oil. We spread butter on bread; the Jew dipped his bread in oil. The earthenware lamp used indoors was simply a saucer of oil on which a wick floated; the torch carried out-of-doors was probably nothing more than a stick with a rag, soaked in oil, tied to the top.

Oil and wine were the main medicines men used. Oil was applied as an ointment to wounds, sometimes with wine added as an antiseptic. It was also used as a base for other ointments. Herod the Great used oil baths to soothe his diseased body. Wine was recommended for faintness, to prevent stomach troubles, and for other kinds of ailments. Wine mixed with myrrh (a bitter, sweet-smelling gum from certain plants) was used to ease pain.

Vineyards and wine-making

WORK IN VINEYARDS was so well-known to everyone that Isaiah could make it the subject of a parable. He tells, for example, how vineyards had to be well protected: strong boundary walls kept out foxes, boars, and thieves.

The branches of the vine were allowed to trail on the ground, but grape clusters were propped up with forked sticks. Sometimes a vine might be supported by a fig tree, so that a man might "sit under his vine." When the grapes had formed, guards were posted in a tower in which they might live until the harvest was over.

The season of grape-gathering was an annual holiday, and whole families moved to the vineyards and camped there. The grapes might be eaten fresh, or dried to eat as raisins. A thick grape syrup known as "honey" was often made by boiling grape juice, but the most common use of grapes was to make wine.

The grapes were spread in the sun for some days before being taken to the wine-press, a square pit cut in rock. There they were trodden by men and women in bare feet, who shouted as they stamped, or sang special songs such as Psalms 8, 81, and 84. The juice trodden out overflowed into a second deeper pit or vat cut in the rock.

In this vat the wine fermented. When, in four days, the "bubbling" stage was over, it was put into earthenware jars. New wine could be drunk after forty days, when the sediment (the "lees") had settled. Wine was separated from the lees by being poured from one jar to another, but usually it was also strained through muslin before drinking.

If the wine was to be sent any distance, it was put into "bottles" made of partly-tanned goatskins. These had been sewed up, leaving one hole to be tied when the skin was filled. Old skins would burst if the new wine was put into them and continued to "bubble"; new skins were elastic enough to stretch a little. Sometimes, however, a hole had to be made even in new skins to let the gases escape.

Wine was drunk every day because water was scarce and not always pure. Old wine was preferred to new because it was sweeter and stronger. It was used at banquets. Wine was valued because it gave pleasure—but drinking too much was considered a great disgrace. Drunkards, Paul said, will not inherit the Kingdom of God.

Fishermen

Fishermen often worked together in their small boats—by night as well as by day. There were several methods of fishing. Sometimes the men fished with baited lines and hooks, but rods are not mentioned in the Bible. Sometimes they fished with harpoons, but this was not common in the time of Jesus. Usually they fished with nets.

Their nets were of two kinds. The first net was a dragnet, rather like the modern seine net. Probably one end was fixed to the shore, and two or more boats arranged it in a circle. The net was supported by floats and weighted at the bottom. In this way, a vast area of the lake was enclosed with a kind of upright wall of net. The other end was brought to shore, and the whole net was pulled in.

IN EARLIER TIMES meat was eaten only at the great religious festivals. Fish, however, was eaten every day, so fishermen were very important people indeed.

In the Bible we do not find any names of particular kinds of fish. The same word could be used for the huge fish which (the story says) swallowed Jonah and for the two small fish carried by the boy at the feeding of the five thousand.

In a way that seems strange to us, all fish with fins and scales were regarded as "clean" and those without (such as catfish and eels) were considered "unclean."

towns on its shores tell us about their connection with fishing. Bethsaida means Fishermen's Houses; Tarichaea means Fish Factory (where fish was cured); Migdol Nunia means Fish Tower (where cured fish was stored).

From these towns fresh fish was carried in baskets to nearby markets, especially Jerusalem—where it was probably sold in a fish market near the Fish Gate. Fish cured at Tarichaea was also sent to markets much farther away—even as far as Rome.

We know that the disciples Peter, Andrew, James, and John were fishermen, and Philip came from Bethsaida. We read that Thomas and Nathanael were eager to go fishing with Peter, so they too may have been fishermen at one time. Why did Jesus choose so many fishermen? Because they were strong and brave and used to working together. They were not rich, always thinking about money and what to buy with it. Nor were they poor, often hungry, and wondering how to make ends meet. So they could think for themselves and judge matters fairly. For these reasons Jesus made them "fishers of men."

The second kind of net was the casting net. A man, working alone, could throw it with a skillful turn of his hand. It was shaped like an umbrella and had weights around the edge.

The Sea of Galilee was famous for its fish, and in the time of Jesus there seems to have been an almost unbroken line of buildings around the sea. The names of many of the

Clothes

On their heads men wore a skullcap or an Arab-style headdress held in place by a ring of cord. Strict Jews had side curls, and most men wore beards, sometimes with moustaches. They usually wore their hair long.

Strict Jews also had little boxes of black leather bound to their foreheads with leather thongs. These contained small pieces of parchment bearing texts from their Bible. A similar box was bound to the left elbow, and the thongs came down to the fingers.

Every woman wore a large head scarf which could be drawn over the lower part of her face like a veil. A widow's veil was black; all others were white. A woman's headdress formed a pad for carrying loads on the head. Women's clothes were similar to the men's but were in brighter colors and decorated with strings of coins or other ornaments.

NEXT TO HIS SKIN a Jew wore a long cotton shirt like a nightshirt. When a fisherman folded this down and was covered only from waist to knee, he was called "naked." When a shepherd tucked the tail of his shirt into the front of his belt so that he could work more easily, he was "girding up his loins."

In later times one could always tell a man was a good Jew because above his shirt he wore a tallith. This was a mantle or short cloak of blue cotton with tassels on each corner. A poor man wore over all a heavy sleeveless cloak which served as a blanket and a raincoat. A rich man wore a long overcoat, open in front and with long trailing sleeves.

Rich women, particularly, were often very vain in their dress. The prophet Isaiah once rebuked them, not only for having so many clothes and fine linen, but also for wearing all kinds of fancy headdress (some "like the moon"), "tinkling ornaments about their feet," leg ornaments, chains, bracelets, headbands, earrings, finger rings, and nose jewels!

Houses and homes

A RICH MAN'S HOUSE, like the one shown below, was usually built of stone. (Our artist has drawn it without its front wall so that you can see into the rooms on this side of the house.) It had many rooms, with one or more for guests. Rich men were always afraid of thieves, for there was no proper police force. For this reason, houses had no windows looking out onto the street. A porter guarded the heavy door leading from the street into the courtyard around which the house was built.

A rich man's house had beds and couches on which to recline at mealtimes. The disciples reclined at the Last Supper, so it was easy for Jesus to wash their feet.

In the time of Jesus, the very rich people might copy their Roman rulers and build a villa. The rich friends of Herod would build their houses in the Greek style.

A poor man's house was square and box-like. The walls were made of mud bricks. Unless the foundations and lower parts of the walls were made of stone, the bricks might wash away in heavy rain. Windows were rare; enough light came from the door; windows would let in only the heat and dust of summer and the cold of winter. The flat roof was made of rough wooden rafters covered with brushwood plastered over with mud.

Except in the rainy season, the roof served as a living room, and stairs led up to it. A law said that a man must build a low wall around his roof.

The house had a little backyard, which was used as an outdoor kitchen. Here stood the oven, where the women baked bread. Here too were the stones they used for grinding flour. There was no fire in the house except when rain drove the family indoors.

In winter the house must have been very crowded; the plow and sickles, the grain ready for sowing, the fodder for the animals, were all brought inside. So were the sheep and goats!

The family sat on a raised platform at one end; the animals occupied the lower part.

There were special ledges in the walls for storing the great rolls of bedclothes—for nights can be very cold in Palestine. Luke tells us about the man who said, "I can't get up to open the door without waking my children who are all in bed with me." The whole family slept together on a large mattress on the floor. When a baby was born, the manger was a handy place for it to lie safe and warm.

Houses were built close to one another for safety. In places a man could walk from roof to roof and talk across the narrow gap to someone on the other side of the street. Thus "to proclaim upon the housetop" was to broadcast what one was saying.

On the doorpost of most houses there was a small box. This was a sign that the owner of the house was a good Jew, for (like the little leather boxes men wore) it contained pieces of parchment bearing texts from the sacred books.

The family

THE "TRIBE" OF ABRAHAM was a group of families who accepted Abraham as their leader or "father." When the Israelites settled in Canaan, each family, under its own father, became more important.

In Old Testament times the father was an all-powerful ruler in his own home: at first with power to punish—even with death—his wife, children, and slaves. (Later, however, his power to punish by death passed to the elders of the town or the king himself.) A woman was seldom expected to think for herself; a daughter had to obey her father; a wife had to obey her husband.

A man might have more than one wife; a woman might have only one husband. In fact, rich men did often have two or more wives, but poor men could afford only one.

A man might divorce his wife and keep the children; a wife could not divorce her husband. The Pharisees asked Jesus his views on divorce. They expected him to side either with the rabbis who taught that divorce was right only where a woman had committed a crime, or with those who said divorce was right for almost any reason. Instead, Jesus said marriages should last forever.

Thus, according to the law, women were regarded as inferior to men, but in practice the wife was usually the respected mother of the family. Jesus, of course, treated men and women as of equal value in God's eyes.

A Jew wanted to have many children, especially boys, so that his family would not die out. He loved his own sons most of all. Jesus loved all children and was angry with his disciples when they began to turn children away from him.

The education of children was important, even though there were no schools almost until the time of Jesus—and then only for boys.

The mother looked after all the children until the boys were about ten years old. During this time boys and girls learned to help their mother in and about the home.

The older girls continued to help her in all the work she had to do. They carried water from the well. They washed clothes in a nearby stream. They learned how to grind corn and bake bread, sticking flat cakes of dough inside the cone-shaped oven over hot red embers. They also learned to prepare vegetables, cook the meals, and spin and weave cloth.

As soon as the boys were old enough and strong enough, they learned to help their father with his flock, in his fields or vineyards, or at his trade.

The mother taught the girls and the younger boys proper rules of behavior. She taught them not only how to pray but also, for example, how important it was to wash their hands before meals. The father taught the older boys. We must imagine the mother and father sitting on the floor or on the housetop with their family around them and telling them stories of the past or explaining the Jewish law.

By the time of Jesus, however, there were schools in every town, and boys began to attend school when they were about six years old. The teachers were the rabbis, and the school was held in their church—called a synagogue—or in the open air nearby. There they sat on the floor around their teacher learning to write and to read the scriptures in the Hebrew language.

What were "cities" like?

IN OLD TESTAMENT TIMES a city might be built for a special purpose—perhaps as a store city or as the headquarters of a chariot army. All cities, however, were places of refuge where people from the countryside could go for protection in winter and in time of war. Usually a city was built on a hill and had strong walls for added protection. Yet by our standards it was only a village in size—where perhaps a thousand people lived in about two hundred houses.

Since it was a place of refuge, a city needed a safe and convenient water supply. Often a city was built on rock, out of which cisterns could be hollowed. These cisterns were sometimes fed by tunnels which brought the water from springs outside the city walls.

There was usually no open space within the walls. Every square foot of ground in the city had houses in it—and they were even built on the wall itself. Houses were built almost on top of each other, and a house higher up a slope might be entered from the roof of one lower down!

There were no main roads except in the largest cities where a broad way might lead to the king's palace or the governor's residence. Streets were narrow, steep, and unpaved. Heavy traffic had to stop at the gates, where there were inns for travelers. People walking through the town kept close to the house walls to avoid the mud and dirt in the center of the alley. In winter, rainwater from the roofs made an alley like a river which scoured out the dirt and rubbish which had gathered there.

The "port," or main entrance, was the most important place in an Israelite city. In war it was the center of the city's defense, with its guardrooms, towers, and double gates.

In time of peace it was almost as important. The space between the double gates was like the marketplace of Roman towns, where city people met their friends and heard all the news from far and near. On the stone benches lining the wall the elders and judges or the king himself would sit and give judgment. Thus "the gate" also came to mean "the law court."

Imagine the crowded scene: beggars crying for alms; peddlers and water carriers shouting their wares; tradesmen arguing over a bargain; singers and storytellers trying to get an audience together. Here, too, laborers are waiting to be hired; a prophet is seeking to be heard; a letter writer sits with his pens. No wonder "the gate" also came to mean the whole life of the city!

By New Testament times life in the smaller towns and villages had not changed very much.

However, foreign conquerors and foreign ways could not be kept out. For more than a century before Jesus was born, Greeks and Romans had been bringing in *their* ways. Parts of the large cities had been rebuilt with fine roads, palaces and amphitheaters, houses and barracks, all built in the Roman fashion. There lived the Roman rulers, their soldiers, and others who copied their ways.

Jesus knew these places, and he passed through cities which looked very much like those of Greece or Rome. The people he spoke to in simple parable-language, however, were mostly the Jews living in little towns and villages in the countryside.

Merchants and craftsmen

On the borders of Palestine, David had conquered lands where there were rich mines of iron and copper—which neighboring countries needed. Then Solomon made a treaty with the Phoenicians, who were great sailors. They not only helped him to build galleys to carry the copper but also provided sailors for them.

Next, the great trade caravans from Egypt to Syria crossed the lands ruled by Solomon, and he made them pay taxes before they could go through his kingdom. This trade was much greater than it had been even in David's day, when goods were still carried on asses. By Solomon's reign, however, more animals from the herds of wild camels in the desert had been tamed. Long camel caravans could carry heavier loads for longer distances. Solomon increased his control of this trade even more when he made a treaty with the queen of Sheba, a small but rich trading kingdom in Arabia which supplied the luxury goods people wanted.

WHEN THE ISRAELITES entered Palestine after the Exodus, they were interested only in farming the land and keeping their flocks.

In the reigns of David and Solomon, however, the kings and some of their subjects began to be much more interested in trade. There were several reasons for this.

What were these goods? They included incense—for use in temples of many religions in many lands; spices to add variety to food; gold, perfume, and sandalwood to add luxury to palaces and rich men's houses.

None of this trade mattered very much to the ordinary Israelite, and prophets pointed out that it did not benefit ordinary people. Moreover, it had a bad effect on the merchants who often copied the pagan foreigners with whom they dealt. So the prophets preached against trade and urged men to be farmers.

This was all very well when Israel was under its own kings, but when foreign rulers owned the land they made life difficult for the farmer. Men found they had greater freedom if they became merchants and craftsmen. So by the time of Jesus, when Israel was under Roman rulers, the rabbis taught that every man *must* teach his son a trade. Among the great rabbis there were woodcutters, smiths, tailors, potters, and cobblers. Jesus was a carpenter; Paul, a tentmaker. Then all work, however humble, was regarded as really work for God.

In some towns, one industry—such as the weaving and dyeing of wool at Magdala—was far more important than any other, but almost every town had a variety of craftsmen for its needs. Usually men following one craft lived and worked in the same part of the town. We know that in Jerusalem there was a "bakers' street," a "valley of craftsmen" (woodworkers and stoneworkers), and a "valley of cheesemakers." There was a "fuller's field" near water where the cloth could be soaked and trampled before being laid in the sun to dry. There was also a "potter's field" where clay was dug. Well away from the houses worked the tanners, because the smell from the tanning of leather was very unpleasant indeed.

Money, weights, and measures

OF COURSE, merchants and housewives needed money, weights, and measures for buying and selling. We read that Abraham bought a cave for four hundred shekels of silver, "current money with the merchant." Coins were not yet used, for a shekel was a weight. Merchants weighed out so much silver for goods, using the quality of silver and the shekel weights accepted in their city.

Money

Long before the time of Jesus, however, coins came into use, and in his day there was Roman, Greek, and Jewish money.

The coin which is most often mentioned in the New Testament is the Roman *denarius*. This was worth about fifteen cents. It was the coin which Jesus called "that which is Caesar's," for it bore the head of the emperor as a guarantee of its value, and it was used for the payment of taxes. A denarius was considered a fair day's wage for a laborer, so we can see how generous the Good Samaritan was when he gave the inn-keeper two denarii. And how lavish was Mary when she anointed Jesus' feet with ointment worth three hundred denarii.

Equal in value to the Roman denarius was the Greek *drachm*—the "piece of silver" in the Parable of the Lost Coin. The woman's ten pieces of silver probably formed part of her dowry and were worn as ornaments. The "thirty pieces of silver" paid to Judas, however, were four-drachm pieces, called *staters*.

The "farthing" which Jesus named as the price of two sparrows was the Roman *as,* worth a little less than two cents. Even smaller than this was the *lepton,* the "mite." When the widow cast her two mites into the offering trumpet of the temple, this was equal to about a half of a cent. Remember, however, she gave all she had.

Jewish coins did not bear "graven images" of any living thing (since this was against their law) but carried pictures of such objects as a helmet or the prow of a ship.

Lepton

Denarius

Stater

Weights

In Old Testament times the Hebrew *shekel* was the common weight and equaled about two-fifths of an ounce. Fifty shekels made 1 *mina* and 60 minas 1 *talent*. In Jesus' day, however, Greek and Roman weights were used—including the *libra* or "pound," which actually weighed about twelve ounces.

Length and area

Goliath, we are told, had a height of six cubits and a span. A *cubit* was a measure based on the length of a man's forearm from elbow to fingertip, about seventeen and a

half inches. A *span* was the distance a man's outstretched hand could cover, from thumb tip to the tip of the little finger—about nine inches. So Goliath must have been nine feet six inches tall.

Two other measures of length mentioned in the New Testament are the *fathom* (about six feet) and the *mile*. This was the Roman mile of 1,000 double paces or 5,000 Roman feet, which would amount to about 1,618 of our yards.

There is no special measure of area mentioned in the Bible. The usual measure was the *yoke*—the amount of ground that a "yoke" or pair of oxen could plow in a day— about two-thirds of an acre.

Capacity

In Old Testament times the *ephah* was used to measure dry goods, such as grain, and the *bath*, to measure liquids. Each was about seven and a half gallons. Ten ephahs made a *homer*, a "donkey-load."

In New Testament times Greek and Roman measures were used. The Roman *sextarius* (about a pint) was one-sixteenth of a *modios* or "bushel," but these words were often used inaccurately. Any small pot might be called a "sextarius." A vessel large enough to cover a light might be called a "bushel." So a man might "hide his light under a bushel."

Jerusalem in the time of Jesus

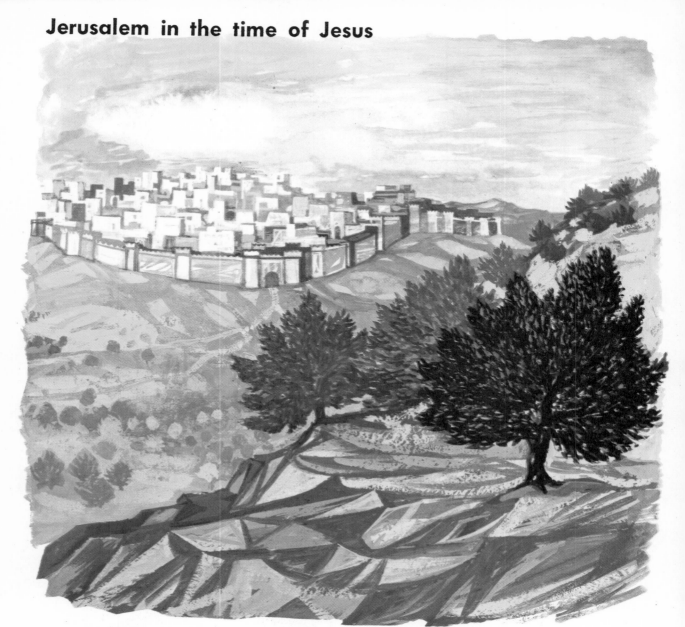

JERUSALEM lies more than two thousand feet above sea level, but on three sides hills rise even higher, overlooking the city and sheltering it. Jerusalem *was* a "golden city," for its walls and towers were built of the warm yellow limestone of the district.

The city was very small by our standards, but it was thickly populated. The streets of the lower city were narrow and very steep. Transport was by donkey or mule, by horse or camel. Rich people might travel in a litter, a kind of couch carried on poles. Shops were open on the street, as they are in the bazaars of India today. As we have read, workers in one craft—such as bakers—usually gathered in one street, their shops side by side. The upper city, in contrast, was a rich district of larger houses and gardens—surrounding the theaters, palaces, and the Temple.

Jerusalem had a plentiful winter rainfall. Every house had a deep cistern in which to store water collected from the rooftop. Two aqueducts carried water from three reservoirs seven miles away. The upper aqueduct took water to the gardens of Herod's Palace, and the lower one to the Temple area, where much water was needed for cleansing.

The only actual spring of water in Jerusalem and the area around the city was at Gihon. It is now called The Virgin's Fountain, from a legend that Mary once washed Jesus' clothes there. The spring was connected to the city by an underground tunnel.

Like the Gihon spring, the Pool of Bethesda was said to have healing powers. It lay north of the Temple, near the Sheep Gate, now called Saint Stephen's Gate. The Pool of Bethesda was arched in by five arches, with five porches on either side of the pool to shelter the sick, and steps down to the water.

For Jesus, Jerusalem was first and foremost the city of the Temple. He made special visits to Jerusalem for the great festivals at the Temple, and almost all the work we are told he did in Jerusalem was done in the Temple area. We shall read later about the Temple and these festivals.

Slaves and masters

EVEN IN THE TIME OF JESUS there were thousands of slaves in Palestine. Every rich Jew had servants—cooks and housemaids, shepherds, gardeners, and so on—who could not leave to go to a better job because they were owned by their master.

How did men, women, and children become slaves in the first place? A man might be a prisoner of war. The slaves employed by Solomon and Herod were almost all captured enemy soldiers.

Some prisoners of war might be sold to private owners. Most slaves in private houses, however, were unfortunate neighbors—such as small farmers or shepherds who had been ruined by bad harvests or by disease in their flocks. A poor man faced with starvation might sell his children or himself and his wife as slaves.

The Bible tells us that in the first place a man became a slave for six years. In the seventh year he and his family could go free if he wished, but if he chose to stay with his master he became the master's slave for life. The fact that men often chose to remain slaves shows that the Jews did not treat their slaves as harshly as other peoples did.

Prisoners of war who were government slaves were treated very harshly, however, and led miserable lives, but there were strict laws about how privately owned slaves were to be treated. For example, slaves had to be given a day off on the Sabbath. If a slave chose to leave after six years, he had to be given presents of animals, grain, and wine (or money instead of these) according to the wealth of his master. In fact, slaves were often treated better than the law laid down, and they were often considered almost as members of the family. They were certainly better off than hired servants, for the master owed these servants only the wages they earned. If they lost their jobs, they might starve.

Why did the Jews treat their slaves better than other peoples did?

First, during the early Israelites' wandering life, men lived and worked together on everyday tasks. No man can treat somebody badly if he is close to him all the time, and so even in Abraham's day slaves were treated well.

Second, the Jews never forgot that their forefathers had been slaves in Egypt for four hundred years. They had toiled in the burning sun to build the wonderful cities and tombs of the Pharaohs. If Jews had been slaves themselves, why should a Jew despise a man simply because he was a slave?

So we find that about four hundred years before Jesus was born, the Book of Job taught that, although some were slaves and others masters, all men should be treated fairly. Jesus not only taught this, but when he washed his disciples' feet (a slave's work), he showed them that nobody need be ashamed of doing work for another—however humble it was. Saint Paul taught that a slave's work was honorable—for was not Jesus the servant of us all?

People have wondered why Jesus did not say that slavery itself was wrong: that because all men were important to God, no man should own another. Jesus was speaking to people accustomed to using slaves, or living alongside them, without seeing anything wrong in it. He did not describe some dreamworld where such customs would cease; he taught people how to treat one another in the real world in which they were living. If they followed his teaching, much of the evil in slavery would wither, and finally the custom would wither too.

31

Pharisees and others

The Zealots wanted to rebuild the nation by actual fighting—by rebelling against the Romans and driving them out of Palestine. There were many Zealots in Galilee and shortly after Jesus was born there had been a rebellion led by a man named Judas. Even one of Jesus' disciples, Simon, had been a Zealot in Galilee.

The Pharisees saw the Law of Moses as a "wall" and tried to keep themselves separate from foreigners and other Jews by living strictly according to the Law. They were very proud of their behavior and advertised it in their showy clothes. Jesus told of a Pharisee who thanked God in public because he was not like other men. Most of the Scribes, the "lawyers" or teachers of the Law, were Pharisees.

BY THE TIME OF JESUS, foreign rulers and conquerors had swept over the natural barriers of mountain and valley, desert and sea. Palestine had been conquered time and again; foreign ways had been brought in by rulers and traders. Many people tried to please their rulers by copying their ways.

Yet most Jews did not want their nation—God's "chosen people"—to be swallowed up by foreign people and their heathen ways. While they were waiting for their Messiah (or Savior) they wanted to begin rebuilding. But they had different ideas about how this was to be done.

32

The men of Qumran actually used the desert as a "wall" when they set up a kind of monastery near the Dead Sea. There they lived, under very strict discipline, calling themselves the "children of light" and awaiting God's Judgment.

Jesus angered all three groups. He angered the Zealots by agreeing that taxes should be paid to Caesar and by saying that the use of weapons was wrong.

He angered the Pharisees when he criticized them for their pride in claiming to be better than other men simply because they obeyed the Law. What was more important, Jesus said, was to try sincerely to become a better man with God's help.

Finally, Jesus angered the men of Qumran when he showed them that men must try to live good lives in the workaday world, not cut themselves off from it.

So none of these men believed Jesus was their Messiah, and even ordinary Jews, the "men in the street," found it difficult to believe he was the Savior they hoped for. Yet, remember, Jesus, too, thought of Israel—most of all the poorer people—as a kind of "vineyard" or "nursery" in which the Kingdom of God could grow.

Jesus, "the Nazarene"

MANY OF THE POORER PEOPLE saw and heard Jesus. Why did they not believe he was their Savior?

True, he was born in Bethlehem, where Micah the prophet had said the Messiah would be born. Its name means "house of bread" or "house of flesh," showing how rich were its fields, pastures, and terraced hillsides.

But everyone thought of Jesus as belonging to Nazareth in Galilee, and they called him "the Nazarene" or "the Galilean." They thought Nazareth a poor place and said, "Can anything good come from Nazareth?" Not that Nazareth was really poor; it was called "Flower of Galilee," and Galilee was a prosperous district. But Galilee was a long way from the Temple at Jerusalem, which made it difficult for Galileans to worship at the Temple as often as they should. Moreover, the people of Galilee spoke with a very strange accent. Surely, men thought, no Messiah could come from there.

Even by a direct way, it was a long walk from Galilee to Jerusalem. To make matters worse, between the two lay Samaria, an "island" of foreigners who had copied the Jewish religion but had not copied the Jews' strict way of life. Jews treated the Samaritans as heathens and believers in magic. When men from Galilee went to the Temple at Jerusalem they usually avoided Samaria and took the long road around the east bank of the Jordan. (See map, p. 2.)

But Jesus taught that Jews should show kindness to Samaritans—which made him unpopular. He even traveled through Samaria. At Jacob's Well, near the town of Sychar, he asked a Samaritan woman for a drink of water. The disciples were astonished to find him talking to a Samaritan—a woman, too!—and asking if he could drink out of the same jar as she used. Then, to their astonishment, he accepted an invitation from the men of Sychar to stay there for a short time.

On his last journey to Jerusalem Jesus chose the long road around Samaria, but on the way he continued to teach how Jews should act towards Samaritans. The last part of this road—the barren stretch from Jericho to Jerusalem—was the setting for the story in which the man who showed kindness was a Samaritan.

Jesus, then, became very unpopular with ordinary Jews when he taught them that men should show kindness to everybody— even Samaritans. He was even more unpopular, however, when he taught that they were mistaken when they hoped to build a powerful Jewish kingdom on earth. *His* "kingdom" was different: it was not an earthly one, and it was not for Jews alone.

So in the end the crowds of ordinary people turned against him too.

Learning to worship God

IN THE TIME OF MOSES, the Israelites had gathered to worship God in a "meeting tent." This must have been much larger than the tents for living in, but in Hebrew it was still called *mishkan*—a dwelling. The translators of our Bible called the meeting tent a "tabernacle" from the Latin word meaning a tent.

Long afterwards men tried to imagine what the tabernacle was like and pictured it as being like their own temple in design and as rich. But all we know for certain is that the tabernacle was larger than other tents and that it contained the Ark.

What exactly was the Ark? The word itself means "a chest" or "a box"—*aron* in Hebrew, *arca* in Latin. This was no ordinary box, however, but the Ark of the Covenant; the sign of God's agreement with the children of Israel. Other people had idols, but God is a spirit; no idol could represent him. The Ark was a plain wooden box carried on poles all the way from Egypt.

No one could see it without remembering how God delivered Israel from Egypt and gave them a land. In the Ark the tablets of the law were kept so no one could see it without remembering that he must keep the

commandments of God—not only the Ten Commandments but the many laws on worship, health, and everyday life later known as "the Law of Moses."

When they settled in the "promised land," the Ark was always kept in one of the "high places" which, with their altars, were centers of worship.

There were many of these "high places," but the one where the Ark was kept for the time being was the most important for all Israel. When David captured Jerusalem he took the Ark there with great ceremony, and the city became the religious capital. Later Solomon built a temple to house the Ark.

Still men worshiped God in the ancient "high places," going to Jerusalem only for some great festival. Sometimes, however, the worship was not well done. At last King Josiah had the "high places" closed and made Jerusalem the only place of sacrifice for all the land. Of course many families living far from the temple could not go there often, and so men met for prayer near their homes.

When their country was overrun by foreigners, the temple was destroyed and with it the Ark. Men learned, however, that what made Israel different from their conquerors was the Law of Moses which they obeyed. When men gathered together to pray and study the law, the place where they met was called a synagogue.

When a new temple was built, there were synagogues in every town and village, too.

A synagogue

IN THIS PICTURE you see one of the Readers standing on the rostrum, a kind of pulpit. He reads from the Hebrew Bible, swaying to and fro as he chants the words. He will be followed by the preacher, who sits while he preaches. The preacher explains in Aramaic (a language they all understand) the meaning of what has been read and adds his comment.

The scrolls of the sacred books are kept on the side nearest Jerusalem in a curtained cupboard which is now called the Ark. Above this, a lamp always burns.

The elders and rulers of the synagogue occupy the chief seats with their backs to the Ark. The seat of honor, called the "seat of Moses," is usually kept for a distinguished visitor. The members of the congregation sit on the side nearest the door, facing the Ark. All wear prayer shawls.

kept. At the regular services, adults were educated in the Law. At the synagogue court the elders punished those who broke the Law. At the synagogue school boys aged six to ten or twelve learned to read the scrolls and to repeat the Law by heart. The Law itself said that parents were responsible for teaching their children, but parents could teach only what they could remember. Only the school in the synagogue (which was often called "The House of the Book") had a copy of the Hebrew Bible from which the written Law could be taught.

In the time of Jesus, women may have taken part in worship at the synagogue; they probably did so outside Palestine. Our picture, however, shows the women in a separate latticed gallery, which was the later custom.

From about four hundred years before Jesus was born, the life of a town or village centered on the synagogue. The life of the synagogue centered on the Book of the Law of Moses and the Ark in which this was

This "written Law" or the "Law of Moses," which every good Jew had to obey, was contained in the first five books of what we call the Old Testament. Later the teachings of the great prophets and some other sacred writings were added to the Book of the Law to make the Hebrew Bible which Jews read today.

39

Herod's Temple

HEROD THE GREAT decided to rebuild the Temple in Jerusalem, to make it the largest and most splendid in the world. The work began twenty years before Jesus was born, and it was not finished when he died.

This new Temple *was* very large. Its outer wall was more than twelve hundred yards long. To make room for it the hilltop was made larger by building supporting arches and great walls made of stone blocks four feet high and fifteen feet long. There were eight gates in the walls and a bridge leading to the center of the city.

The Temple *was* very splendid. It was built of white marble, and the walls of the Sanctuary were overlaid with beaten gold. There were many carved pillars, and around the Outer Court ran splendid porches.

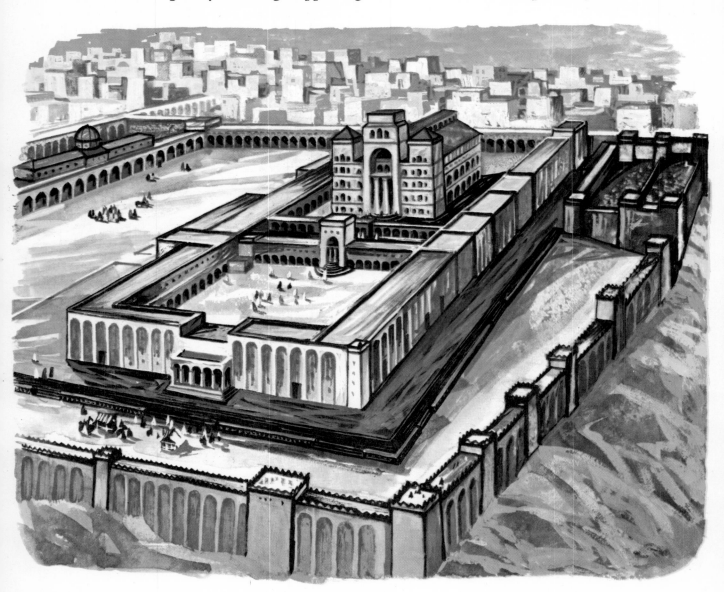

The courts rose one above the other; above the Outer Court was the Court of the Israelites, and the Sanctuary rose above that. The porch into the Sanctuary was very high, so that the eyes of worshipers were drawn upward.

All this reminded men that only the best is good enough for God and that only those willing to climb may worship God. But another lesson taught by the building was that only certain kinds of people may draw near to God. This lesson was taught by means of different walls.

The outer wall was high and spiked. The next wall, at the foot of fourteen steps, was low, but on it were notices in three languages reading, "Any non-Jew passing this boundary will be responsible for his own death which will certainly follow." The next wall marked the limit to which women might enter, and the next was as far as ordinary men might go. Only priests might pass this wall to the altar of burnt offering where they made sacrifice.

The Sanctuary was divided by a curtain. The first part, sixty feet long, was the Holy Place where priests, chosen by lot, entered to serve the Altar of Incense. The second part, thirty feet long, was the Holy of Holies which only the High Priest could enter, and only on one day of the year. The Holy of Holies was in darkness except when it was lit by the seven-branched candelabra, and it was empty. For God is a spirit; no idol could ever represent him.

The meaning of the walls is still true; only a certain kind of person can draw near to God. But Jesus said that the test is not, "Are you a Jew, or a male, or a priest?" The test is, "Are you pure in heart?" "Do you love God and love your neighbor?"

Today some of our churches are open for worship only one day a week. The Temple was open every day for worship and sacrifice.

Early each morning a priest stood on the highest pinnacle of the Temple to watch for the dawn. He then gave the sign for the morning sacrifice to start, accompanied by the blaring of silver trumpets. The whole city heard and rose to pray. At twilight evening offerings were made with prayer. In synagogues throughout the world at that very hour, similar words were spoken, so that every Jew—all over Palestine and in foreign lands—might know that his prayers mingled with those in the Temple.

Harvest festivals

As we have already seen, when the Israelites conquered Canaan they learned how the Canaanites farmed the land. They also learned that the Canaanites made sacrifices to their god Baal—to please him and to ensure that their farming was successful.

It is not surprising that the Israelite farmers felt they should give thanks to their God in similar ways. They took the three great Canaanite festivals and gave them a new meaning by adding old customs of their own.

The first festival in the year was a thanksgiving to God for the grain harvest standing in the fields ready to be cut. In earlier times the main act of this festival was a ceremonial waving of the first sheaf of barley cut. Until this offering had been made it was not lawful to reap or to use any part of the new crop for food.

Another part of the festival was the sacrifice of a lamb. This was a common sacrifice by shepherd people and one the Israelites had practiced for ages. In later times this part of the festival became the more important because it recalled the great days of the Exodus. We shall read more about the Feast of the Passover.

The second festival was the real Festival of Harvest. It was later called the Festival of Weeks because it began after the seven weeks of harvest—that is, on the fiftieth day after the sheaf-weaving ceremony.

The festival marked the end of the grain harvest by offerings of loaves of bread made from the new crop. At this time men also began to make their own offerings of "first-fruits"—the first portion of each of their own crops. Thus they showed thanks to God as the giver of the land and all that grew on it.

The last festival of the year was the Festival of the Ingathering, which marked the end of the grape harvest. It was the gayest of all three.

Pilgrims who went to Jerusalem for this festival first collected branches of myrtle and willow from the outskirts of the city. With these they made shelters in which they ate and slept for all seven days. (This reminded them of the forty years in the wilderness when the Israelites lived in tents or shelters.) Twigs from the branches were bound together to form a *lulab* which, with a citron, was carried in procession and waved as a sign of joy.

There were three ceremonies on each of the seven days of the feast. First, there was a special morning service at the Temple, when water was splashed over the altar as a sign of thanks to God for the gift of rain.

Then followed the night-long ceremony of lights and dancing. Four huge lamps lit the Temple area while men carrying torches danced to the music of flutes. As the men danced, priests sang the Psalm of Ascent (Psalms 120 to 134)—one on each of the fifteen steps between the Court of the Israelites and the Court of the Women. We can be sure that all over the land there were similar rejoicings in which women also took part.

Finally, at dawn, the third ceremony was performed. The priests gathered at the east gate of the Temple area. As the sun rose, they turned to face the Temple, crying out, "Our fathers when they were in this place turned with their faces toward the east, and they worshiped the sun toward the east: but as for us, our eyes are turned toward the Lord."

The Passover in the time of Jesus

The first part of the Festival took place at the Temple. There, instead of the usual one division of priests, all twenty-four divisions were on duty. The usual afternoon sacrifice was made an hour earlier than usual. Three hours after noon the Levites sounded the trumpets three times to mark the beginning of the sacrifice of the Passover sheep.

Each family now brought its sheep to be killed. Some Levites sang the Hallel or Song of Praise (Psalms 113 to 118). Others caught the blood in gold or silver vessels and poured it on the altar, representing the life offered to God. Others skinned and dressed the sheep and burned some of the fat, again as a sign of thanks to God.

To CELEBRATE the feast of the Passover, families flocked to Jerusalem from all over Palestine and from every land where Jews were settled. A hundred thousand pilgrims—or more—crowded into this small city, where every room was full, and the shopkeepers enjoyed a great rush of business.

Each family kept the Festival together. But since each group sharing the feast had to number at least ten people, neighboring families or several branches of one family might share a room and a sheep. Probably they arranged at the previous Passover for a room of a suitable size. When they arrived at Jerusalem, they had to buy a sheep of a suitable size too. It had to be large enough, because each had to receive a piece at least the size of an olive—but not too large, as the whole sheep had to be eaten the same day. Wine and spices had to be bought also.

Now each sheep was wrapped in its own skin and carried to the room where the "family" waited for the second part of the Festival. In a portable clay oven the sheep was roasted on a spit of pomegranate wood, with its legs still unbroken and with its head folded into the space where its stomach had been.

The meal was served at low tables. The family, all dressed in white, reclined on cushions on the floor. After the blessing of the food, the first cup of wine was shared by the whole family. Then the lamb was eaten with bitter herbs dipped in a paste of mixed fruits and nuts called *harosheth*. After a second cup of wine, the "son" of the group asked the question, "Why is this night different from all other nights?" This was the signal for them to recite, in song and story, the long history of God's saving of Israel, beginning with the first Passover. The recital ended with a prayer for the deliverance of Israel from Roman rule.

Jesus in the Temple

In this same Outer Court, or Court of the Gentiles, the money changers set up their tables. Nearby stood the stalls and pens of the traders who sold animals and doves for the Temple sacrifices, as well as oil and salt for special parts of the ceremonies.

It seems strange to us that part of a temple should be a market, but to a Jew the Court of the Gentiles was not really part of the Temple. In any case, this Outer Court was large enough to give plenty of room for the traders and money changers to work at one end without disturbing the rabbis' schools which met at the other. The Temple police made sure that the traders did not make a nuisance of themselves.

Moreover, the money changers were useful. The pilgrims probably carried only Roman money, and the "tribute" or money offering they paid every year had to be given in coins which did not bear a "graven image." They changed their Roman money at the money changers' tables.

JESUS HAD BEEN familiar with the Temple all his life. He was only about six weeks old on his first visit to the Temple. Mary had taken him from Bethlehem to "present him to the Lord," as all Jewish mothers presented their eldest sons. This presentation must have taken place in the Court of the Women, since both Mary and Anna, a prophetess, took part. When he was twelve years old, Joseph and Mary took him to Jerusalem for the Passover and he attended one of the schools of the rabbis, which were usually found in the Outer Court, under one of the covered arches.

We also know that when he was a man he was present at several of the great Festivals at the Temple, and that he taught the crowds then thronging the Outer Court of the Temple. Later, Solomon's Porch became a favorite place for the disciples to meet.

The traders in animals, too, were useful. Only the best animals—male, "without blemish," and preferably red in color—were acceptable. The priests who inspected the traders' animals allowed them to sell only those they approved as up to the required standard. It was, therefore, far safer to buy these approved animals than bring in others.

Then why did Jesus drive the money changers and traders out, overturning their tables, and angrily telling them they were turning the Temple into "a den of thieves"?

Because they were making too much profit out of the pilgrims. To make matters worse, they were working for the High Priest and members of his family. The money changers charged too much for changing Roman money; the traders charged as much as ten times the prices pilgrims would pay for animals outside. Worse still, people knew that priests often declared falsely that animals bought outside were "blemished" or not good enough. The priests did this to make sure there was enough trade for the High Priest's servants.

So Jesus was popular with the people when he "cleansed" the Temple of this greed and cheating. Although the High Priest was furious, he dared not do anything. Remember, however, that Jesus respected the Temple itself. He worshiped there, and taught there, but when he saw abuse he removed it.

Finding out more . . .

THE BEST PLACE is, of course, the Bible itself. Almost every story in the Old and New Testaments tells something about the way people lived and thought.

The long story of Abraham (Gen. 12 to 25) tells us how the ass-nomads lived. We can read, for example, about how they traveled with their flocks (Gen. 13:1–11), fought over precious water places (Gen. 26: 20–22), and welcomed guests (Gen. 18: 1–8).

When Jesus called himself "the good shepherd," (John 10:1–16) he was not thinking of a meek and gentle man, but of a tough character who was not afraid to tackle wild beasts to protect his flock. Jacob described the tough life of a shepherd in Gen. 31: 38–40. It was as a shepherd that David learned his courage and skill to kill Goliath (I Sam. 17:34–36). Some rules for shepherds are listed in Exod. 22:10–13.

Farming was familiar to all people—even tradesmen and fishermen, who worked in their own small fields. The Book of Ruth (Chapter 2) describes a typical harvest scene. The parables of Jesus are full of pictures taken from farming life. Read, for example, Matt. 13:1–9, 24–30, and 31–32.

Fishing was not so familiar to everyone. Jesus told parables about fishing only when he spoke from a fishing boat on the Sea of Galilee (Matt. 13:47–48).

The story of the wise and foolish bridesmaids shows the use of oil for lamps (Matt. 25:1–13), while the story of the Good Samaritan shows its use for healing (Luke 10:29–37).

Jesus knew the need for good foundations for a house (Matt. 7:24–27), but the roof of brushwood and mud could easily be broken up (Mark 2:1–12). The "roof chamber" of Elisha (2 Kings 4:10) shows what an honored guest might expect in his time.

We read of the smith in Isaiah 54:16 and (of Philistine smiths) in 1 Sam. 13:19–21; of the weaver in Job 7:6; of the potter in Jer. 18:1–4; of the tanner in Acts 9:43.

Of course there is a great deal of detail in the Old Testament about worship. The perfect tabernacle, which men later imagined, is described in Exod. 26 and 36:8–38 and the temple of Solomon in 1 Kings: 6 and 7. The festivals are described in the ancient "calendars" in Exod. 23:14–17, 34:18–23; Deut. 16:1–17.

For a Jew the greatest day of a week was the Sabbath (Exod. 31:14–15) about which the Pharisees were so strict. Jesus observed the Sabbath (Luke 4:16) but said "the Sabbath was made for man" (Mark 2:27) and the breaking of the Sabbath laws was less important than the need to love your neighbor (Mark 3:1–6). Jesus criticized the Pharisees because they cared too much for appearances (Matt. 6:1–21, 23:1–12) and not enough for their fellowmen.

Finally, read again the story of the first Christmas in Luke 2:1–19. Can you picture the scene more clearly now?

PRINTED IN U.S.A.